MW00947071

Copyright © 2024 by J.L. Holden

All rights reserved.

No portion of this book may be reproduced in any form without written permission from the publisher or author, except as permitted by U.S. copyright law.

THANKFUL BEAR

A Fall and Thanksgiving Book About Gratitude for Toddlers and Children

J.L. Holden

In a little red house
in a forest of
orange, yellow and green
lives a very nice
bear family.

There's Papa Bear
And Mama Bear
And Sister Bear
And Thankful Bear.

"Thankful Bear,"
you say.

"Why that's a
funny name."

But if you
knew him,
you'd call him
the same.

For Thankful Bear
is thankful all the time.
He looks for anything
to be thankful for
anything he can find.

No matter what
every day
wherever he is
you'll hear
Thankful Bear
say...

I'm thankful for the breeze.

I'm thankful for the trees.

I'm thankful for all their colorful leaves.

I'm thankful for play time.
I'm thankful for friends.

I'm thankful for stories
even The End.

I'm thankful for our neighbor Fox.

I'm thankful for jumping rocks.

I'm
even
thankful
for all of these socks.

I'm thankful for scarves.

I'm thankful for cars.

I'm thankful for warmth.

I'm thankful for cool.

I'm thankful I get to go to school.

I'm thankful
for mama
who hugs me
real tight

and teaches
me music
until I play it
just right.

I'm thankful
for every thing
that I learn.

I'm thankful
when sister
waits for
her turn.

I'm thankful for pumpkins and apples too.

I'm thankful for acorns, the sun and the moon.

There is just
so much
to be
thankful for.

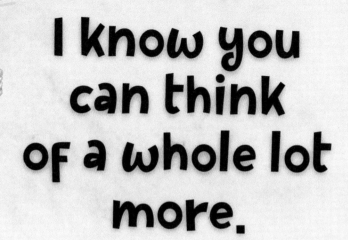

I know you can think of a whole lot more.

mom & dad
my sister
our home
grandma
grandpa
my room
books
the sky
the ocean
the forest
the river
love
the stars
learning

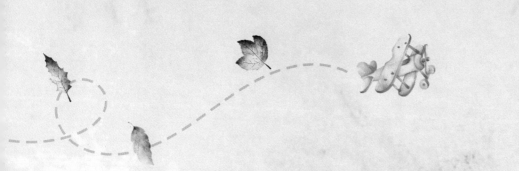

Really you can.
Here's what to do.
Listen real close
and
I'll share it with
you.

Whenever I wake up, I start right away looking around for something to say

I'm thankful for you.

And do you know what?
It makes my heart happy.
That is a fact.

By just being thankful
for this and for that.

So, look for it always
and
everywhere.

THANKFUL

Then
you'll be
like me,
Thankful Bear.

The End

THANK YOU FOR READING THANKFUL BEAR. IF YOU LOVED THIS STORY PLEASE CONSIDER LEAVING A REVIEW TO HELP OTHERS FIND IT.

ALSO BY. J.L. HOLDEN

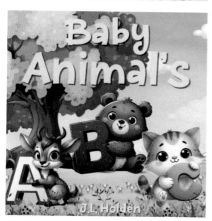
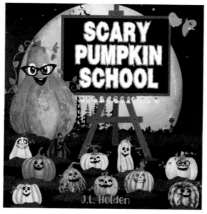

Made in the USA
Las Vegas, NV
24 November 2024

12578818R00021